Children's Authors

Norman Bridwell

Jill C. Wheeler
ABDO Publishing Company

visit us at
www.abdopub.com

Published by ABDO Publishing Company, 4940 Viking Drive, Edina, Minnesota 55435.
Copyright © 2005 by Abdo Consulting Group, Inc. International copyrights reserved in all
countries. No part of this book may be reproduced in any form without written permission from
the publisher. The Checkerboard Library™ is a trademark and logo of ABDO Publishing Company.

Printed in the United States.

Cover Photo: Getty Images
Interior Photos: Corbis pp. 7, 9, 17, 21; de Grummond Children's Literature Collection,
    University of Southern Mississippi Libraries p. 18; Getty Images p. 23; Norman Bridwell
    pp. 5, 15

Editors: Heidi M. Dahmes, Jennifer R. Krueger
Art Direction: Neil Klinepier

Special thanks to Norman Bridwell for providing photos for this project.

Library of Congress Cataloging-in-Publication Data

Wheeler, Jill C., 1964-
    Norman Bridwell / Jill C. Wheeler.
      p. cm. -- (Children's authors)
    Includes bibliographical references (p.) and index.
    ISBN 1-59197-605-7
    1. Bridwell, Norman--Juvenile literature. 2. Authors, American--20th century--Biography--
Juvenile literature. 3. Children's stories--Authorship--Juvenile literature. 4. Dogs in literature--
Juvenile literature. [1. Bridwell, Norman. 2. Authors, American. 3. Illustrators. 4. Authorship.]
I. Title. II. Series.

PS3552.R44535Z73 2004
813'.54--dc22
[B]
                                                                    2003063843

Contents

He's Red and He's Warm

Most children have heard of Clifford, the big red dog. Clifford is in almost every public library and toy store. He is a well-meaning dog. But, he's just so big he often gets into trouble.

Writer and illustrator Norman Bridwell created Clifford. Since 1962, Bridwell has written more than 40 Clifford books. He created two other series as well. More than 100 million copies of his books have been printed.

The Clifford books have been translated into several languages, including Chinese. Clifford is now known around the world. Sometimes readers know him by other names. He is Ketchup in France and Bertram in Canada. In Germany, children know him as Samson.

Young readers love Clifford because he makes mistakes just like they do. However, he is often only trying to be helpful. He and Emily Elizabeth love each other no matter what. That is what many readers think is most important.

Bridwell explains his reason for continuing the Clifford books all these years by saying, "I love the kids. You couldn't think of a better audience to write for."

Meet Norman Bridwell

Norman Ray Bridwell was born on February 15, 1928, in Kokomo, Indiana. His father, Vern, worked in a factory. His mother, Mary, was a homemaker. Norman was just over a year old when the **stock market** crashed in 1929. This marked the beginning of the **Great Depression**.

Many people lost their jobs and their savings during the Great Depression. Norman's family struggled as well. They didn't have a lot of money for extra things.

Norman sought comfort in books. He remembers reading *The Bears of Blue River* as a child. The book is the story of pioneer life in Indiana Territory. It describes the many struggles the early settlers faced. Their stories of hardship made Norman's life seem much better.

Norman made up stories when he was not reading them. He often entertained himself with these stories on the way to and from school. He invented entire imaginary kingdoms. He also acted his stories out with toys. Sometimes he drew pictures of the characters in his imaginary kingdoms.

Drawing was one of Norman's favorite hobbies. Yet, he admits others did not think he was very good at it. There was always someone in his class that was better than him. But, he did not let that stop him from doing what he loved.

A covered bridge near Kokomo, Indiana

Struggling Artist

Norman decided to study art after high school. He entered the John Herron Art Institute. The institute was in Indianapolis, Indiana.

Norman spent four years studying art at the institute. He then moved to New York City. There, he took classes at another art school. It was called Cooper Union Art School.

After Cooper, Norman began his art career. He went to work as a **commercial artist**. Norman also worked running errands for a **lettering** company for a while. He then went to work for a fabric company in New York City for two years. There, he designed fabrics for neckties.

His next stop was the H.D. Rose Company. The H.D. Rose Company hired Norman to design cartoons for slides and **filmstrips**. Norman spent three years there before deciding to start a new career. He wanted to be a **freelance artist**.

Norman studied art for one year at Cooper Union Art School in New York.

In June 1958, Norman married a fellow artist. Her name was Norma Howard. She did watercolors, oil paintings, and **prints**. Norman and Norma soon had two children. Their names were Emily Elizabeth and Tim.

Story in a Sample

Being a **freelance artist** was hard work. Bridwell was always working to find new assignments. Sometimes he had a hard time finding enough work. Bridwell decided in the early 1960s that he needed to make extra money. He thought he might do it by illustrating children's books.

He started by creating some sample illustrations. Then, he began visiting publishing houses. Bridwell went from publisher to publisher showing his drawings. However, none of them had any work for him.

Finally, Bridwell talked with an editor at Harper & Row Publishing. She told Bridwell it would be hard for him to publish a book of illustrations. His artwork was not good enough to stand alone. The editor suggested Bridwell write a story to go with his drawings.

The editor then flipped through Bridwell's sample pictures. She pointed to one. It was a small girl and her red bloodhound. The dog was nearly as big as a horse. The editor told Bridwell he might be able to make a story from that picture.

Bridwell began work on his story right away. He kept the dog red. He also decided to make the dog even bigger so the story would be funnier.

Opposite page: *Bridwell says, "Clifford does what you'd like to do but can't. Because Clifford is so big and also because he's a dog, he's able to do the most unbelievable and imaginative things."*

Hello, Clifford

Bridwell had visited with the editor on a Friday. He spent the weekend turning his dog picture into a complete story. Bridwell made it about the kind of dog he had wanted as a child, only bigger. He named the dog's owner Emily Elizabeth after his own daughter.

By Monday, Bridwell had a book called *Clifford the Big Red Dog*. Then, he crossed his fingers and gave the **manuscript** to a publisher. The publisher was Scholastic Press.

Three weeks later, Bridwell received a phone call. Scholastic wanted to publish the book. *Clifford the Big Red Dog* hit bookstores in 1962. Bridwell warned his wife that he probably would not sell any more books.

Bridwell was wrong. Scholastic published his books *Zany Zoo* and *The Cat and the Bird in the Hat* in 1964. In 1965, he produced a **sequel** to his Clifford book. He called it *Clifford Gets a Job*.

Scholastic editors decided to stop the Clifford series after the second book. Neither book had sold many copies. Later, members of the company changed their minds. They reissued the first Clifford book as part of their popular school book club program.

Bridwell was asked to create two more books about the giant dog. He wrote *Clifford Takes a Trip* and *Clifford's Halloween* in 1966. The Clifford series was off and running.

Bridwell was ready to name his giant dog Tiny. However, Norma thought Tiny was not a strong enough name. She suggested he name the dog after an imaginary playmate she had as a child. Her playmate was named Clifford.

13

Happy Accident

Bridwell has learned a lot in his years of writing. He learned it is hard to guess exactly what editors want. He discovered this when he first set out to become a children's book illustrator.

Bridwell had been spending weeks on another Clifford book. He decided to take a break the night before he was to show the **manuscript**.

He played around sketching a new story about a witch. She was a nice witch who struck up a friendship with her young neighbors. He called the story *The Witch Next Door*. He thought he would show it to the editors as something extra.

The editors loved *The Witch Next Door*. They did not like the new Clifford book. Still, Bridwell walked away with another published book. *The Witch Next Door* went on to become one of Bridwell's most popular books.

Bridwell has done several books based on the character in *The Witch Next Door*. He has also done a series of books based on funny monsters. The monster books include jokes and riddles. Sometimes Bridwell also draws the pictures for books written by other authors.

Bridwell once said, "Sometimes you'll do something that you really like and no one else does. You'll feel terrible, but you've just got to press on and keep trying."

Clifford Everywhere

Bridwell gained a new group of fans in 1972. That year, he wrote and illustrated *Clifford the Small Red Puppy*. It was the first of many books in the Small Red Puppy series. The books were later made into **board books** for very young readers.

Bridwell used the Clifford the Small Red Puppy series to help preschoolers learn. Some of the books help with counting. Others help with colors, numbers, and shapes. There are also Clifford pop-up books and activity books. Clifford is on tapes, CDs, and videos, too.

Clifford became even more famous in 1989. The Macy's Thanksgiving Day Parade in New York City featured a giant Clifford balloon. Bridwell wrote about the balloon in a 1993 Clifford book. It is called *Clifford's Thanksgiving Visit*.

In 2000, Clifford moved from books to television. The Public Broadcasting Service (PBS) launched an **animated** Clifford series. The series included Clifford and Emily Elizabeth, but it also introduced some new characters. They live on imaginary Birdwell Island. Birdwell is a play on Bridwell's name.

Clifford flies at the 1989 Macy's Thanksgiving Day Parade. Bridwell says that **Clifford's Thanksgiving Visit** *is his favorite Clifford book.*

Bringing Clifford to Life

Bridwell still loves to draw Clifford. He feels very fortunate to be working on something that he enjoys so much.

Bridwell uses the same process when creating each book. He creates rough pencil

Original pencil illustration from **Clifford the Big Red Dog**

sketches when he first gets an idea. Then, he shows the sketches to his editor. He makes ink drawings when the first sketches are approved.

Another artist colors in Bridwell's sketches. However, Bridwell gets to suggest the colors. Finally, he writes the text for the book. It takes him about three months to do a new book.

Bridwell likes talking to children about writing and drawing. Sometimes he does interviews over the Internet, too. Bridwell likes to share an important lesson with young writers. He tells them not to give up when their work is rejected. Bridwell says if writers enjoy writing and keep at it, they will succeed.

When exploring ideas for Clifford books, Bridwell draws what is funny to him.

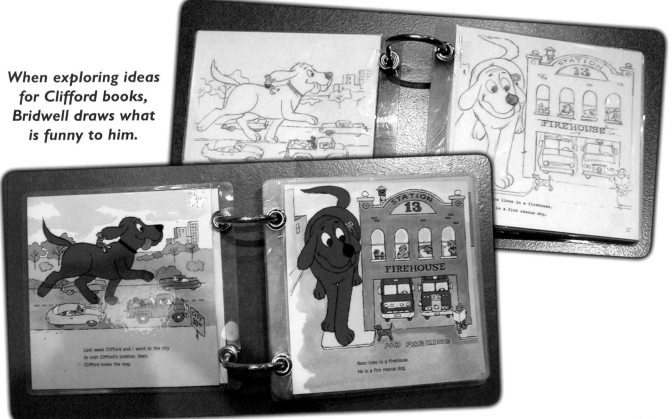

Making Kids Laugh

Bridwell published his first Clifford book when he was 34 years old. He is now in his 70s. He never expected to be so successful. He admits his books are not the best ones out there. However, kids and their teachers love them. He enjoys writing stories that make kids laugh.

Bridwell and his family now live on Martha's Vineyard in Massachusetts. Bridwell enjoys several hobbies when he's not writing. He likes to read. He also likes doing crossword puzzles and going to plays.

And of course Bridwell is still writing and drawing. He says coming up with new book ideas is getting harder for him. Writing the text can be difficult. Drawing the pictures is the easy part for Bridwell.

In fall 2003, Bridwell got some help with new book ideas. He judged a writing and drawing contest. It asked children to tell what they would do with a big red dog. They had to write a story or send in a drawing.

Opposite page: *Laura Bush reads a Clifford book to children in Uganda.*

Bridwell picked the winning entry and will use it in a future Clifford book. He still enjoys reading letters from young readers. And, his books remain a favorite of children and teachers.

Glossary

animation - a process involving a projected series of drawings that appear to move due to slight changes in each drawing.

board book - a book made up of cardboard-like pages. These books are designed for toddlers and preschoolers.

commercial artist - an artist who does work for businesses rather than galleries.

filmstrip - a strip of still pictures that can be projected on a screen.

freelance artist - an artist who does work for different employers. They do not become an employee of one company.

Great Depression - a period (from 1929 to 1942) of worldwide economic trouble when there was little buying or selling, and many people could not find work.

lettering - the design of letters.

manuscript - a book or article written by hand or typed before being published.

print - a reproduction of an original work of art.

sequel - a book or movie continuing a story that began previously.

stock market - a place where stocks and bonds, which represent parts of businesses, are bought and sold.

Web Sites

To learn more about Norman Bridwell, visit ABDO Publishing Company on the World Wide Web at **www.abdopub.com**. Web sites about Norman Bridwell and Clifford are featured on our Book Links page. These links are routinely monitored and updated to provide the most current information available.

Index